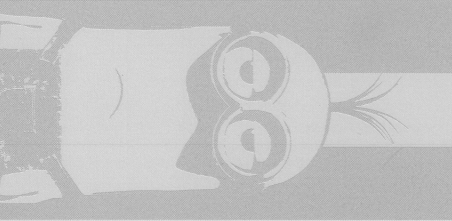

MINIONS 2016

A CENTUM BOOK 978-1-910916-29-2

Published in Great Britain by Centum Books Ltd

This edition published 2015

2015 © Universal Studios Licensing LLC.

1 3 5 7 9 10 8 6 4 2

Minions is a trademark and copyright of Universal Studios. Licensed by
Universal Studios Licensing LLC. All rights reserved.

TM and © Universal Studios.

Centum Books Ltd, Unit 1, Upside Station Building, Solsbro Road,
Torquay, Devon, TQ2 6FD, UK

books@centumbooksltd.co.uk

CENTUM BOOKS Limited Reg. No. 07641486

A CIP catalogue record for this book is available from the British Library

Printed in Italy

minions

2016

centum

Contents:

This book is bursting with Minions, dinosaurs, villainous plans, vampires, jewels, pirates, royalty, Egyptians, a yeti, bananas and . . .

BELLO!

YOU HOLD IN YOUR HANDS THE ULTIMATE GUIDE TO THE MOST CLEVER, MISCHIEVOUS, ACCIDENT-PRONE, LOYAL AND BANANA-LOVING MINIONS OF ALL TIME. READ ON IF YOU WANT TO LEARN HOW TO SURVIVE THROUGH THE MOST DANGEROUS PERIODS OF HISTORY, NO MATTER HOW MANY DESPICABLE MASTERS YOU LOSE!

LOOK FOR THE BANANA HIDDEN ON EVERY PAGE.

ADVENTURE OF A LIFETIME

Are you ready for the adventure of a lifetime? Do you want to know how the Minions evolved through the ages, to serve the most despicable masters throughout history?

You'll need a guide to show you what's good – or bad! These three yellow fellows may look cute and cuddly but they know what every despicable master is looking for and there's guaranteed adventure along the way!

Draw pictures of all the snacks and treats you will pack into your lunchbox for the adventure of a lifetime!

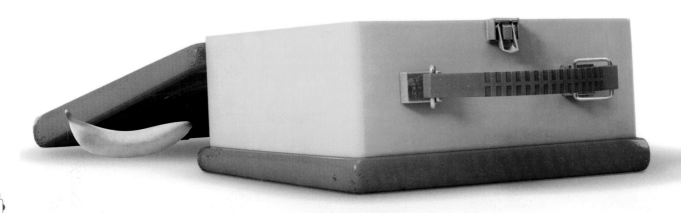

Bob, Kevin and Stuart would like to share their journey for a new despicable master with you. Pack your bag and let the search begin!

BOB KEVIN STUART

JOIN THE TRIBE

It's time to reveal your inner yellow – draw yourself as a Minion! Choose your hair, colour yourself yellow, and add a pattern to your overalls. Then fill in all your Minion info.

Draw some 'interesting' hair to help you stand out. Remember you're one in a **MINION!**

Hello
my name is

Minions go by many names so there's a lot for you to choose from: **Dave, Carl, Norbert, Kevin . . .**

"Blumock!"

"Big Boss"

"Bello!"

Write some things about yourself as a Minion here.

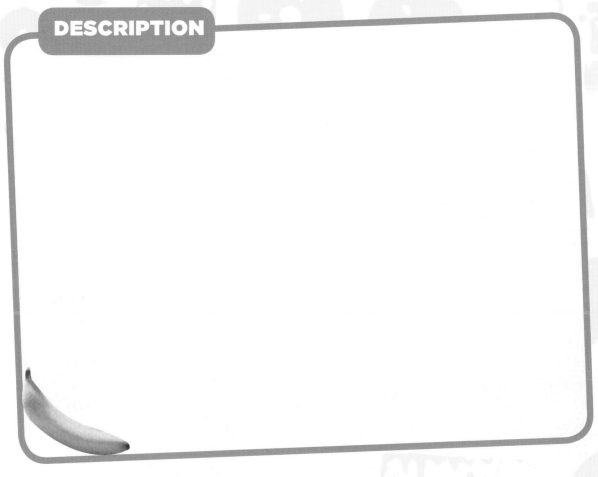

DESCRIPTION

Every single Minion in the tribe has a special talent, whether it's seal training or solo ping pong! What's yours?

SPECIAL TALENT

MINIONS:
STORY OF THE MOVIE

Minions have been on Earth since the beginning of time. They want just one thing: to find the biggest, baddest master to serve.

Keeping a master wasn't easy – at first each master was eventually replaced – or eaten – by a bigger, badder boss.

When they finally left the sea, the Minions found the giant T. rex. It was love at first sight . . . until they accidently knocked the T. rex into a volcano!

Whoops!

During the Stone Age mankind emerged. The Minions took an instant liking to man and wanted to serve him well. When a bear came after him, they handed the man a flyswatter to fend off the bear.

It seemed like a good idea – it wasn't. The bear won the fight.

Next, the Minions found a pharaoh in ancient Egypt who asked the Minions to build his pyramid. But the Minions built it upside down; it fell over, squashing their master flat.

But Minions do not give up.

They found another master in the Dark Ages – Dracula.

Who knew if they opened the curtains the sunlight would turn him to ash?!

Then the Minions nearly killed Napoleon with a poorly aimed cannon blast. His army pursued the Minions for hundreds of miles.

They finally found refuge in a cave. Here they forged their own civilisation.

At first it was fun. But with no leader to serve, the Minions had no purpose.

But all was not lost. For one Minion had hope.

His name . . .
. . . was Kevin.

Kevin revealed his big plan to his buddies. He would leave the cave and find the biggest, baddest master for the Mionions to serve. But he needed help.

"Me coming!" Bob yelled.

Kevin looked down at Bob; he was the smallest Minion and Kevin worried that Bob was not strong enough for the dangerous journey ahead.

Thankfully a Minion in the back raised a ukulele in the air. It was a sleepy one-eyed Minion named Stuart, whose friends were playing a trick on him.

Stuart stood up, and joined Kevin, not really sure why everyone was clapping for him.

Bob was Kevin's only other option.

"Ugh . . ." Kevin huffed. "Komay."

Bob grabbed his teddy bear Tim and was ready to go.

MINIONS:
STORY OF THE MOVIE

"Big boss! Big boss!" chanted the tribe as Kevin, Stuart and Bob walked towards the cave exit and off to find their new boss!

The journey was treacherous. They hiked over mountains, through the dense forests and paddled across an ocean in a canoe.

They slept. They got hungry, and food was scarce. Stuart became so hungry he imagined Bob and Kevin were bananas and started licking them! But then they saw a beautiful woman in the distance. And she was . . . green?!

It was the Statue of Liberty. Kevin, Stuart and Bob had reached New York City in all its 1960s glory.

First things first, they needed new clothes and Kevin spotted something perfect, denim and blue . . .

"*Bueno!*" Stuart said, turning round so he could see his reflection in the glass window. His bum looked good . . . really good.

Then they took off through the streets, dwarfed by the giant buildings, hot-dog stands and even the fire hydrants . . . by everything, really.

Bob got distracted by a woman in a banana-print dress and followed her into a taxi. Stuart and Kevin searched for their lost friend. Finally they spotted him going into a department store and followed him. Suddenly the lights went out. The Minions wandered around to find that the store was closed. They'd be stuck inside for the night.

Kevin found a big bed with a TV in front of it. They huddled together and switched on the TV.

Stuart wiggled the antennae, until suddenly a man in a black suit appeared on the screen. "You're watching the top-secret Villain Network Channel," he said. "If you tell anyone, we'll find you."

There were pictures of a giant convention with different villains.

"VNC is sponsored by Villain-Con. For eighty-nine years the biggest gathering of criminals anywhere," the man said. "Plus a special appearance from the first female super villain . . . Scarlet Overkill!"

A woman's silhouette appeared on screen. Even her shadow seemed menacing.

This was it . . . the master they'd been looking for.

"Get to Villain-Con this weekend. Only at 545 Orange Grove Avenue in Orlando, Florida," the announcer said.

Kevin stood up, jumping on the bed. "Villain-Con! Orlando! La big boss!"

Kevin, Stuart, and Bob needed a ride to Orlando, wherever that was. As they walked along a road, leaving the city, Kevin picked up a piece of cardboard and wrote *Orlando* on it. It wasn't long before a car came towards him and screeched to a stop.

"All aboard the Nelson Express!" the man inside bellowed. The Minions scrambled in and were on their way to Villain-Con with the Nelson's, a loving family of criminals.

After hours of driving, "we're here," yelled Walter, "Villain-Con!"

The Minions looked out of the window. The car was moving into an underground convention hall.

"Villain-Con!" Stuart cried. "La Villain-Con!"

All around was a sea of villains of all shapes and sizes.

Kevin pulled Stuart and Bob towards the hall. This was the moment they'd been waiting for. Scarlet's voice boomed, "Doesn't it feel so good to be bad?" Then, she burst through the screen and used her jetpack dress to rocket around the hall.

"Have any of you ever dreamed of working for the greatest super villain of all time? Well, what if I told you that I am looking for new henchmen?"

The Minions felt like they were going to explode. Kevin rubbed his ears. Did she just say she needed new henchmen?!

"It's just a matter of proving you're good enough," Scarlet went on. "Just take this ruby from my hand and you've got the job . . ."

Hundreds of villains rushed towards Scarlet. She whirled round and sent them flying backwards off the stage.

Kevin looked at the pile of defeated henchmen. The Minions wanted to serve the biggest, baddest boss, but they wanted to leave intact!

Just then, Bob's teddy bear Tim slipped from his hands and was kicked across the stage and Kevin saw the ruby thrown high in the air.

When Scarlet had fought off the last of the villains, she looked around.

"Didn't my speech inspire anyone?" she yelled. "All these villains and I still have the . . ." Scarlet realised that she didn't have the ruby. Instead she was holding Bob's teddy bear. "Who has the ruby?" she shrieked.

Bob coughed and spat the ruby onto the floor.

Scarlet smiled. "The job has been filled!" She whisked Kevin, Stuart and Bob into her sleek, futuristic red jet, and they set off.

GETTING TO KNOW
KEVIN

TAKES INITIATIVE

He's a Minion with a plan to find the tribe a new evil master to serve.

NAME: Kevin

CHARACTER TRAITS: Proud "big brother", not so great at public speaking

BEST BITS:
Playing polo on a corgi
The discovery of the Minions' blue overalls
Leading the Minions to their perfect master

LOVES: Protecting his buddies, spending time with Stuart and Bob, epic adventures, flying in Scarlet's jet, heists, Villain-Con, police chases, the Nelson family

HATES: Disappointing his Big Boss

What do you like most about Kevin?

_____

Kevin's using his noodle again – draw his next big idea in the bubble.

Perfect pic:

Minion 101:
Au Naturel

Minions have always served the most despicable masters throughout time, including T. rex who roamed the prehistoric world terrorising the other dinos and just being mean – the perfect villainous master.

DID YOU KNOW?

- The first dinosaurs lived on Earth **230 million years ago**. They ruled the Earth for the next **160 millions years**!

- Scientists think there were at least **1,500 different species of dinosaur**.

- Many of the best-known dinosaurs would never have met because they lived during **different eras**. For example a T. rex could never fight a Stegosaurus because they were **separated by about 80 million years**.

- The word **'dinosaur'** means **'terrible lizard'** in Greek.

What to wear

There's nothing more *naturel* than an outfit made of leaves!

Create clothes from leaves

Vines to hold leaves in place

Fashion goggle straps from – you guessed it – more leaves!

THE MASTER FILE: T. REX

T. rex was the perfect evil master – he was mean, had an awesome roar, and he was so big that the whole tribe could ride on his back!

The Minions thought they had won the jackpot after millennia of following around evil fish. But the Minions found his weakness – T. rex can't handle the heat of a fiery volcano!

QUICK QUIZ:

1. Dinosaurs only ruled the earth for 160 years.

True or **False?**

2. What does *dinosaur* mean in Greek?
a. 'Terrible dog'
b. 'Terrible master'
c. 'Terrible lizard'

3. How many species of dinosaur do scientists think existed?

ANSWERS ON page 60

21

GETTING TO KNOW
STUART

He didn't know it, but Stuart was born for adventure! Thank goodness he took that nap and got volunteered to join Kevin on his mission.

NAME: Stuart

CHARACTER TRAITS: Cool, musical, flirt, hungry

BEST BITS:
Falling in love with a yellow fire hydrant
Loves to eat bananas!
Rocking out in front of Buckingham Palace

LOVES: Playing his ukulele, hot tubs

HATES: Snow globes

What do you like most about Stuart?

_____

Is this Stuart's shadow, or has he picked up a shadowy impersonator on his travels?

Perfect pic:

ANSWERS ON page 60

23

MINION 101: CRO-MINION

The Stone Age rocked for the Minions. There were cool caves to live in, exciting new tools and interesting accessories. Their new human master was brave . . . very brave . . . sometimes too brave for his own good. The Minions learned this the hard way during a unfortunate incident with a bear and a flyswatter.

DID YOU KNOW?

- Human ancestors, *Homo sapiens,* emerged around **200,000 years ago**.

- *Homo sapien* means **knowing man**.

- **The dog** was the first animal to be **domesticated**. They were used to protect humans from danger, to help with hunting and to provide warmth on chilly nights – stinky!

- Early humans **painted the walls of their homes** with paints made from animal fat and crushed-up bones.

Minions take style very seriously, and the Cro-Minion was no exception.

Who said a tool can't be made of wood?

Accessorise with bones

Match the colours of your fur and accessories carefully. Choices are brown, brown and, er . . . brown!

THE MASTER FILE: CAVEMAN

When Minions met man they knew they were on to a good thing. Although man was shorter and hairier than T. rex, he was much smarter. Unfortunately, early man was apparently quite delicious to bears.

QUICK QUIZ:

1. Early humans drew pictures on their cave walls.

True or **False?**

2. What sort of animal did cavemen cuddle up to?

_____

3. What does *Homo sapien* mean?
a. 'Dancing man'
b. 'Knowing man'
c. 'Hunting man'

_____

ANSWERS ON page 60

ROBERT.
BOBBY
my BOY

Bob loves adventures and exploring and making new friends and, well, everything! That's what makes him so lovable.

NAME: Bob

CHARACTER TRAITS: Overly excitable, sweet, loyal, lovable "little brother"

BEST BITS:
Making Tim dance when asked for special skills at the evil henchmen placement stand
Swallowing the red ruby
Pulling the sword from the stone

LOVES: His teddy bear Tim, giggling, playing hide-and-seek, making friends

HATES: Bees, being away from his buddies, losing Tim

What do you like most about Bob?

_____

Perfect pic:

How many times can you see the name 'TIM' in the letter grid below?

T	I	M	I
I	M	I	T
M	I	T	I
T	I	M	M

ANSWERS ON page 60

MINION 101: EGYPTIAN

Ancient Egypt was an exciting new time for the Minions. At last a people who were as obsessed with their powerful masters as the Minions were! They should have fit right in! The Minions were trusted with important jobs, like pinning the blueprints up the correct way . . . uh-oh!

DID YOU KNOW?

- Most ancient Egyptian pyramids were built as **tombs for the pharaohs** (who were the rulers of ancient Egypt) and their families.

- Over **130 pyramids** have been discovered in Egypt.

- Both Egyptian men and women **wore make-up**. As well as offering protection from the sun, the Egyptians believed make-up had magical healing powers too.

- The Egyptian alphabet contained **more than 700 symbols** called **hieroglyphs**. Imagine learning over 700 letters!

Ancient Egypt was hot, hot, hot! And these yellow fellows grabbed the chance to keep it cool and simple!

Carry a pot. Even if you don't need to!

Curly pointy toes are so authentic

A snazzy leather strap perfectly complements Minions' goggles

THE MASTER FILE: PHARAOH

The Minions' pharaoh master seemed perfect; he was sophisticated, smart and had a giant pyramid built to ensure he was remembered for all time.

One thing their pharaoh did not plan for was the Minions reading the blueprints upside down and finding out a bit too late – whoops!

QUICK QUIZ:

1. Why did the ancient Egyptians build pyramids?

_____

2. How many symbols (hieroglyphs) did the ancient Egyptian alphabet have?
a. Over 700
b. Over 100
c. Over 70

_____

3. Only ancient Egyptian women wore make-up.

True or **False?**

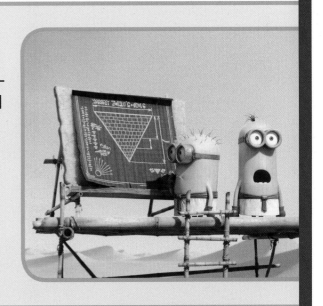

ANSWERS ON page 60

MINION 101:
GONE BATTY

When the Minions met Dracula they felt right at home. His Transylvanian castle was simple but comfortable. The Minions set to work on their look to coordinate with their new master. Dracula was a party animal, but only at night though! Sadly, the Minions forgot this golden rule and . . . POOF!

DID YOU KNOW?

- Dracula means '**son of the dragon**'.

- Transylvania is an actual place in **Romania**.

- Vampires like to **sleep all day** and **stay awake all night**.

- Vampires **cannot be exposed to sunlight**.

The Minions really adopted the Transylvanian vibe when it came to their uniform.

Giant collars create a spooky look

Fake fangs make a Minion fit right in

Floor-length cape because they look so scary

THE MASTER FILE: DRACULA

The Minions loved working for Dracula. He stayed awake all night and slept all day.

The Minions decided to throw him a special bash for his 357th birthday. But when they pulled back the curtains to reveal his cake, he turned to dust!

1. Vampires cannot be exposed to starlight.

True or **False?**

2. Transylvania is a place in which modern-day country?

_____

3. Dracula means 'son of the _____'
a. Bat
b. Wolf
c. Dragon

_____

ANSWERS ON page 60

MINION 101: EYE, MATIE

Avast, me hearties! Life at sea was a dream come true for the Minions: mingling with salty sea dogs, searching for treasure and doing jigs to pirate songs – what could be better? Plus the outfits were awesome! If only they hadn't gone on that fishing trip . . .

Did you know?

- Pirates had many **superstitions** and believed that piercing their ears would improve their eyesight.

- About 300 years ago, thousands of pirates sailed the seas and oceans in the '**golden age of piracy**'.

- The most famous pirates had terrifying reputations; they advertised this by flying the '**Jolly Roger**' flag with its picture of skull and crossbones.

- Pirates used **compasses** and the **stars** to navigate their ships.

What to wear

Being Minion to a pirate master requires sensible clothing. A pirate Minion must be ready to somersault from a rope and lift a chest full of treasure at any moment!

ALWAYS carry a sword: the bigger the better

Extra-strong leather belt

The rule for hats, like swords, is always go big if possible!

The master file: pirate

The Minions took their pirate master into their hearts. Like them, he was misunderstood in many ways and spoke in a language almost as incomprehensible as their own.

It was unfortunate for everyone that the shark thought the Captain looked so tasty!

QUICK QUIZ:

1. How long ago was the 'golden age of piracy'?

2. Pirates believed that piercing their ears would improve their eyesight.

True or **False?**

3. What did pirates use to navigate their ships?
a. Compasses and stars
b. Sat navs and smart phones
c. Minions

ANSWERS ON page 60

MINION 101: VIVE LE MINION

The Minions thought things were going so well with Napoleon and his army. They always made sure they were in full military uniform and had been given some VERY important jobs, like cannon-firing duty. But when it went wrong, it went terribly! The Minions were chased into exile in the icy wasteland of the polar ice cap!

DID YOU KNOW?

- Napoleon's nickname was **Little Commander**.

- He once wrote a **romance novel** called *Clisson et Eugénie*.

- Napoleon was rumoured to have a **fear of cats**.

- After being exiled on an island, he **escaped** and took over Paris again.

The French are masters of style and the Minions' Napoleon uniform is no exception.

A stylish plume with matching cuffs is a must!

Small weapon? No problem, just pull a good face

Shoulder belts – they just look good!

THE MASTER FILE: NAPOLEON

Ah Napoleon – short, power-crazy and fond of conquering countries.

The Minions thought they'd found their perfect master, at last a leader they could see eye to eye with – literally! But then it all went . . . BOOM!

QUICK QUIZ:

1. What was Napoleon's nickname?

_____

2. Napoleon was afraid of dogs.

True or **False?**

3. What was the name of Napoleon's romance novel:
a. *Claude et Clisson*
b. *Clisson et Eugénie*
c. *Clisson and Peter*

_____

ANSWERS ON page 60

35

Scarlet's jet travelled so fast it wasn't long before they reached England and her castle in the middle of London. "Herb! My baby!" Scarlet called inside. She hugged her husband, a sleek inventor named Herb.

"Herb, these are the new recruits: Kevin, Stuart and Bob," Scarlet said.

"Right on." Herb laughed. "You guys are crazy little and way yellow and I dig that!"

Scarlet looked seriously at the Minions. "Okay, listen up! It's time to get down to business." She pointed to a painting. "This is Queen Elizabeth," Scarlet said, "Ruler of England, and I really, really want her crown. Steal me the crown and all your dreams come true. But if you fail, I'll blow you off the face of the Earth. OK?"

Kevin, Stuart and Bob went to Herb's lab. They needed gadgets to help them. In the lab the Minions saw a large metal machine.

"When it's finished it'll be my Ultimate Weapon," Herb told them. "So, you're here for gear . . ."

The Minions nodded.

Herb looked down at Bob. "You get my Far-out Stretch Suit."

"Stu," Herb said. "Behold the Hypno-Hat!"

The next morning the Minions went to the Tower of London to steal the queen's crown. They sneaked inside as a group of guards approached.

Stuart pushed the button on the side of his Hypno-Hat. The guards were hypnotised and started to dance around. The Minions ran past the guards and towards the back entrance of the Crown Jewels room.

Kevin blasted a hole right through the steel. There was the queen's crown. The Minions ran as the display case lowered into the floor.

The crown was taken by the queen's guards into a horse-drawn carriage. The Minions ran to catch it up.

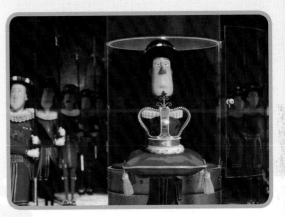

Bob activated his Stretch Suit. He made his legs two stories high, grabbed his friends, and ran after the carriage.

He flung Kevin and Stuart inside the queen's carriage.
"Gimme la crowna!" Stuart yelled at the queen. Hundreds of police chased after the carriage. "After them!" the queen shouted.

Bob ran all the way to a square and grabbed a sword that was wedged into a giant boulder. The crowd fell silent. The clouds above parted, casting Bob in a heavenly glow.

It had long been said that no one except a true king could pull the sword from the stone. But now Bob had done it. He was the new king of England!

MINIONS:
STORY OF THE MOVIE

A reporter stood outside Buckingham Palace. "One of England's most famous myths has become a reality," he said, talking into a camera. "Bob has pulled the famed sword right from its stone and is the new king."

Scarlet was watching the news. "Tiny yellow traitors!" she shouted at the TV.

At the palace, a line of guards, on Bob's request, were all wearing yellow outfits and goggles.

"Awwwww buddies!" Bob yelled. He'd only been at the palace for a few minutes, but it already felt like home.

The Minions were playing in the great hall. Kevin hit a polo ball across the room. Just then, the door swung open. The ball smacked Scarlet Overkill right on the nose.

"How dare you!" she yelled, her face red.

"You little traitors!" she fumed. "You stole my dream! I was going to be made queen and you pinheads screwed it up!"

Kevin plucked the crown from Bob's head and gave it to Scarlet, trying to make amends.

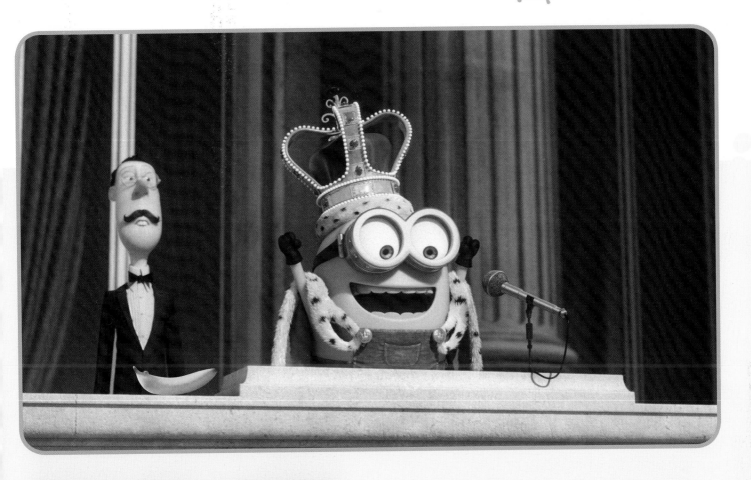

The Minions took everyone into the Houses of Parliament, where Bob as king declared Scarlet as the new queen of England. "La keena pota Scarlet po papiel!" Bob shouted.

Scarlet turned to the Minions. "Come with me," she said. "You're finally going to get everything you deserve."

The Minions skipped through the palace. This was it – finally their master would reward them for all their hard work. Scarlet led them to some stairs at the far end of the palace. Kevin, Stuart and Bob had only taken a few steps, when Scarlet slammed the door behind them. Slowly their eyes adjusted to the dark. Metal torture devices covered the walls. She'd locked them in the palace dungeon . . .

ICE SPY

It's the Minion Choir! Beautiful singing, freezing cold temperatures and, unfortunately, a torn picture! Can you find the missing pieces that complete the picture of these musical Minions?

a
b
c
d
e
f
g
h

ANSWERS ON page 60

MINION GELATO CONES RECIPE

If, like the Minions, you want ice cream even when it's freezing, then this is the perfect recipe for you! It's not ice cream though, it's a banana, chocolate, marshmallow mash-up! I bet the Minions wish they'd thought of that!

INGREDIENTS:

2 bananas

4 tablespoons of chocolate spread

A handful of mini marshmallows for each cone

4 ice cream cones

Ask an adult for permission and help before you start this **YUMMY, SCRUMMY SPECIAL TREAT.**

INSTRUCTIONS:

1. Peel the banana and place it in a bowl.

2. Now add the chocolate spread to the bowl.

3. Use a fork to mash the banana and chocolate spread together.

4. With a spoon, divide the mixture into four and pack it into the ice cream cones.

5. Push the mini marshmallows into the mixture on top of the cone.

6. Place the ice cream cones into the freezer for one hour.

Now there's nothing left to do but enjoy. And make your friends feel super jealous that they haven't got one!

TIE-DYE PARA TÚ

Follow the instructions so you can look like a groovy peace-loving hippy Minion from the 60s with your own tie-dye T-shirt!

COVER ALL WORK SURFACES AND WEAR SOME OLD CLOTHES in case things get messy!

ASK FOR AN ADULT'S PERMISSION AND THEIR HELP before you start this cool creation!

YOU WILL NEED:

1 pack of coloured dye
A squeezy bottle
500ml of warm water per dye colour
An old cotton T-shirt
Large plastic bag
Large plastic bowl or sink
Rubber gloves
Elastic bands or string

INSTRUCTIONS:

1. Wash the T-shirt and leave damp.
2. Pinch the centre of the T-shirt and pull up into a cone shape.
3. Using the elastic bands, tie every four centimetres from the end of the cone.
4. Put on your rubber gloves and dissolve the dye in 500ml of water or follow the instructions on the packet.
5. Put the dye solution into a squeezy bottle.
6. Place the tied T-shirt into the empty plastic bowl and apply to the selected areas straight from the bottle.
7. Once complete, put the T-shirt in a plastic bag, seal it and leave overnight.
8. Without untying the fabric, rinse in cold water until the water runs clear, then untie and wash in warm water.
9. Dry and dazzle all your friends with your cool and groovy style!

WARNING: The first few times you wash your tie-dye T-shirt, wash it separately from other clothes in case there is any excess dye.

Colour this guy's T-shirt to look like yours!

GETTING TO KNOW SCARLET

She is the world's first female super villain and she's coming to rob a museum near you!

NAME: Scarlet Overkill

APPEARANCE: Impeccably stylish! 1960s beehive hairdo, red dress, long black gloves

CHARACTER TRAITS: she's committed to getting what she wants.

BEST BITS:
Entrance into Villain-Con 1968
Being crowned queen of England – almost!
Sending her dress into 'attack mode'

LOVES: Rubies, Herb, her trophies of crime, the British royal family (especially their jewels!).

HATES: When her henchmen fail her.

MODE OF TRANSPORT: The Scarlet Jet

MOST LIKELY TO SAY: "DOESN'T IT FEEL **GOOD** TO BE **BAD?**"

Perfect pic:

What is Scarlet planning to steal now? **DRAW A PICTURE IN THE BUBBLE.**

GETTING TO KNOW HERB

He has some of the coolest gadgets of the swinging 60s. If you want some super-stretchy arms just because it's groovy, then Herb's your man.

NAME: Herb Overkill

APPEARANCE: Cool hair, cool suit – he's simply cool!

CHARACTER TRAITS: He loves Scarlet and her crazy criminal ways!

BEST BITS:
Giving Kevin, Stuart and Bob some awesome gadgets to help them steal the crown
Hanging in his hanging chair!
Thinking up new names for everyone

LOVES: Scarlet, inventing gadgets, soup, romance, explosions.

HATES: Not much! This groover is a peace-loving hippy at heart.

MOST LIKELY TO SAY: "YOU GUYS ARE CRAZY LITTLE AND WAY YELLOW, AND I DIG THAT!"

Perfect pic:

Part of inventing great gadgets is thinking up groovy new names for them. Some of Herb's inventions include: the Hypno-Hat and Far-out Stretch Suit. **USE THIS SPACE TO WRITE DOWN SOME NAMES FOR YOUR INVENTIONS.**

HELLO, LONDON

Kevin, Stuart and Bob have found a new master, yay! All they have to do now is try to make her happy . . . not easy! Their mission is to steal the queen's crown but they don't know where to start looking.

Help them travel across London as quickly as possible on the tube, to reach a telephone box and look for clues. Add the minutes at each circle along each different coloured line to find the quickest route.

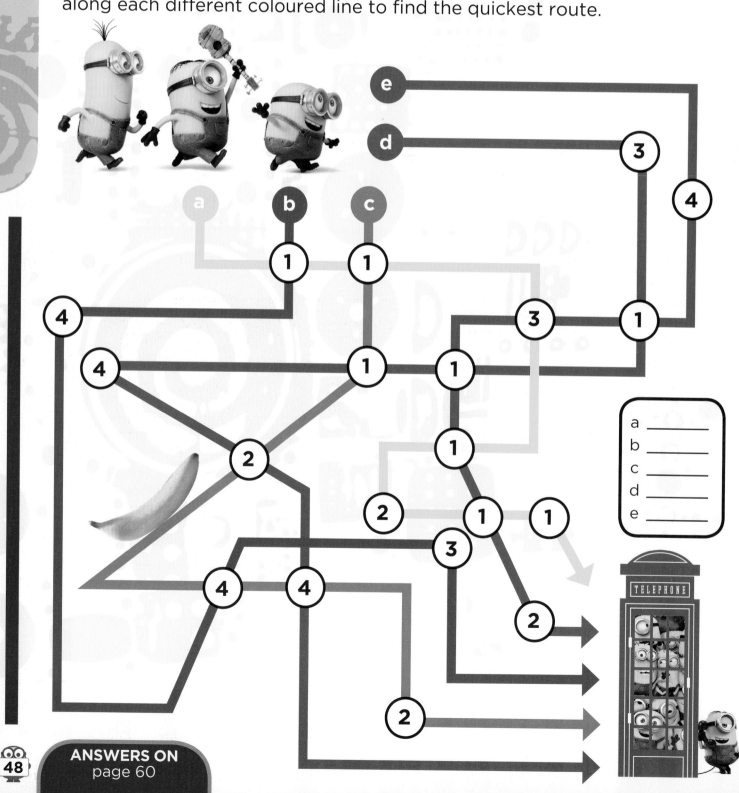

a _____
b _____
c _____
d _____
e _____

ANSWERS ON page 60

PAY CLOSE ATTENTION!

More than anything else Scarlet hates it when her Minions don't pay attention. So she has prepared a test for you: study this picture for one minute, then turn the page and answer as many questions correctly as you can. No pressure, but Scarlet expects perfection!

PAY CLOSE ATTENTION!
QUESTIONS

Now answer as many questions as possible about the picture on the previous page.

1 Which hand was Herb holding up?

_____

2 What can you see in the portrait that appears to be next to Scarlet?

_____

3 Did you see Scarlet's legs in the picture?

_____

4 What colour was the jewel on top of the crown?

_____

5 How many emeralds were visible on the crown?

_____

6 What colour was Scarlet's dress?

_____

7 How many buttons did Herb have done up on his jacket?

_____

8 What colour was Herb's belt buckle?

_____

9 Was Herb wearing a tie?

_____

10 What colour was the wall in the room?

_____

HOW MANY DID YOU GET RIGHT?

NOW TEST YOUR FRIENDS AND SEE IF THEY CAN BEAT YOUR SCORE!

BRITISH BLOOPER

Never have so many posters, created by so few Minions, made so little sense to so many people. These posters are a mess! They each have one word missing. Use the pictures found on each poster as clues.

KEEP
CALM
AND
WAVE
A
GLAF

KEEP
CALM
AND
CARRY
A
DORSW

KEEP
CALM
AND
CARRY
A
REBA

KEEP
CALM
AND
PLAY
LOOP

KEEP
CALM
AND
WEAR
A
KRITS

KEEP
CALM
AND
WEAR
A
ROCWN

ANSWERS ON page 60

They crawled out of the sewer next to where Scarlet was being crowned. The doors were locked. They would have to climb inside the cathedral.

Inside the cathedral the Minions saw Scarlet standing below them.

Suddenly a bee started circling Bob's head. Stuart and Bob were forced on to the chandelier. The bee chased the Minions in circles. Stuart and Bob kept running, trying to get away from it, but the more they ran, the more unsteady the chandelier became. The screw that held it to the roof came loose.

Far below, Scarlet smiled as the archbishop stepped forward with the crown. "I proclaim thee, with great reservation, the queen of England!"

Hearing the commotion, Scarlet looked up just as the chandelier fell from the ceiling. Kevin managed to grab Stuart and Bob before it plummeted to the ground and landed on top of Scarlet.

The Minions hadn't meant to hurt Scarlet, but they knew that this did not look good!

Suddenly they heard a crash. Scarlet shot up towards the ceiling. She had been protected by her dress – a new state-of-the-art villain suit that Herb had designed. She hovered, staring at the Minions, her face red with rage.

She pointed at the Minions. "Get them!" she shouted to the crowd.

The Minions ran, trying to lose the angry villains. But villains emerged from everywhere. Kevin got separated from his friends. He kept glancing back, but he couldn't see them anywhere.

Kevin kept running, until he saw a television set. A reporter was speaking into the camera, until Scarlet pushed him out of the way.

"Kevin, I know you're out there!" she screeched into the camera. "Look what we have here!"

She reached down, pulling up Stuart and Bob. They were both tied up.

"Buddies!" cried Kevin.

He had to help his friends!

Kevin broke inside Herb's lab; he needed supplies! He tumbled into Herb's Ultimate Weapon and activated it. "Three . . . two . . . one . . ." said a mechanical voice. The machine started to work. Kevin grew . . . and grew . . . until he was thirty stories tall.

"Buddies!"

he cried and he stomped off to find them.

Stuart and Bob sat tied to sticks of dynamite. "This is it, boys," said Scarlet.

They struggled against the rope, watching in panic as the fuse burned lower and lower . . .

Wham!

A giant boot slammed down on the fuse, snuffing it out.

"Bello!" Giant Kevin cried out.

Kevin tried to free his friends, but someone was behind him. "So that's your plan?" Scarlet shouted as she flew behind him. "Make yourself a bigger target?"

Just then Kevin noticed a huge crowd on the other side of the street. It was his buddies – not just Stuart and Bob, but all of them. They had travelled across the globe to find their missing friends and now they were ready to fight with Kevin.

"This ends now!" Scarlet growled.

Scarlet's dress activated into its final stage, revealing a nuclear core. She aimed the bomb at the Minions and fired. Kevin took a step forward, leaned in . . . and swallowed it.

"Have fun exploding!" Scarlet cackled.

Scarlet scooped up Herb and flew off. She wanted to get as far away as possible. Kevin grabbed them and was dragged along. The beeping inside Kevin sped up. The bomb was about to go off. "No, no, no, no, no!" Scarlet cried.

Booooooooooooom!

MINIONS:
STORY OF THE MOVIE

The Minions watched in horror as the sky was filled with smoke. It took them a moment to notice the speck of yellow in the sky.

"Looka!" Bob cried, showing the other Minions. It was Kevin floating back down to earth, using his blue overalls as a parachute and he was back to his normal size.

The Minions had done it – they had saved all of London from Scarlet Overkill, the tyrant queen. But Scarlet's story wasn't over quite yet . . .

Scarlet and Herb hurtled through the sky until they crashed in the middle of a snowy wasteland.

"Where are we?" Scarlet said.

She looked up and saw several angry-looking yetis. Scarlet wasn't intimidated. Within hours, she became their queen. It was the coronation she always wanted.

Life works in mysterious ways. Scarlet and Herb finally had a kingdom to rule. It didn't have a castle, but it was air-conditioned.

In London, Queen Elizabeth addressed a giant crowd. "We are here today to celebrate the Minions. The country owes you a great debt of gratitude."

"Bob," the Queen went on, "you were wise and noble king for all of eight hours. So for you, I offer this tiny crown for your teddy bear Tim."

"Tri makasi! Tri makasi!" Bob cried, jumping up and down in excitement.

"Stuart," the Queen continued, "for you I have this beautiful snow globe." Stuart looked at the glass globe in his hand, trying hard to smile. It was a strange present.

"Just joking!" the queen laughed. "Don't be mad at me – it was Kevin's idea." Then Kevin stepped forward with a beautiful red electric guitar for Stuart.

"Coolos!" Stuart said, smiling.

"Kevin!" the queen said. "You are a hero of the highest order. For your bravery and valour, I am knighting you. From here on out, you are Sir Kevin. Well done."

"Kevin! Kevin! Kevin!" all the Minions chanted. They carried their leader on their shoulders, into the streets of London. Kevin had saved the day and won the love and respect of his tribe.

MINIONS:
THE QUIZ

1. Can you identify each master?

2. Put these masters in the correct historical order.

Napoleon   Caveman

Dracula   T. rex

Pirate   Scarlet Overkill

Pharaoh

3. When and where are these pictures from?

4. Know your Minion:

a. Which Minion loves to play the ukulele?

_____

b. Which Minion swallows Scarlet's ruby?

_____

c. Which Minion has his head nibbled in the boat to New York?

_____

_____

5. Know your master:

a. Which master got eaten by a shark?

_____

b. Which master got blown up?

_____

c. Which master fell into a volcano?

_____

d. Which master got taken for a nuclear ride with Kevin?

_____

6. Who's that?

ANSWERS ON page 60

IT'S TIME FOR ANSWERS

DID YOU FIND THE BANANA HIDDEN ON EVERY PAGE?

PAGE 21
1. False
2. c
3. Over 1,500

PAGE 23
No. The shadow does not match Stuart's picture.

PAGE 25
1. True
2. Dogs
3. b

PAGE 27
7 times

PAGE 29
1. As tombs for their pharaohs
2. a
3. False

PAGE 31
1. False
2. Romania
3. c

PAGE 33
1. About 300 years ago
2. True
3. a

PAGE 35
1. 'Little Commander'
2. False
3. b

PAGE 40
'c', 'g' and 'h'

PAGE 48
The yellow line is the fastest.

PAGE 50
1. His right hand
2. A vase of flowers
3. No
4. Blue
5. Two
6. Scarlet, of course!
7. Two
8. Gold
9. Yes
10. Purple

PAGE 51
1. Flag
2. Sword
3. Bear
4. Polo
5. Skirt
6. Crown

PAGE 58–59
1. a. Pirate
   b. Scarlet Overkill
   c. Caveman
   d. T. rex

2. T. rex, Caveman, Pharaoh, Dracula, Pirate, Napoleon, Scarlet Overkill

3. a. Ancient Egypt
   b. Time of the dinosaurs
   c. New York City, 1960s
   d. London, 1960s

4. a. Stuart
   b. Bob
   c. Kevin

5. a. Pirate
   b. Napoleon
   c. T. rex
   d. Scarlet Overkill

6. a. Herb Overkill
   b. Walter Nelson
   c. Tim the bear

04273386